ARMOURED TRAINS 1921–1939

STRATUS

ADAM JOŃCA

POLISH ARMOURED TRAINS 1921-1939

VOL. 2

Published in Poland by
STRATUS s.j., ul. Żeromskiego 6A
27-600 Sandomierz, Poland
e-mail: office@mmpbooks.biz
as MMPBooks
e-mail:rogerw@mmpbooks.biz
© 2023 MMPBooks
http://www.mmpbooks.biz
Copyright © 2023 Adam Jońca
Copyright © 2023 Stratus s.j.

ISBN
978-83-67227-36-0

Editor in Chief: Roger Wallsgrove
Editorial Team: Bartłomiej Belcarz, Artur Juszczak, Robert Pęczkowski
Author: Adam Jońca
Cover: Dariusz Wyżga
Layout Design: Bartłomiej Belcarz
Translation: Artur Przęczek
Proof-reading: Konrad Przeczek

Printed by
Wydawnictwo Diecezjalne
i Drukarnia w Sanodmierzu
www.wds.pl

PRINTED IN POLAND

Photographs: the author's collection, Tomasz Basarabowicz, Bogusław Bobel, [the late] Pascal Danjou, Jacek Haber, Artur Przęczek, Sławomir Kordaczuk, Dariusz Kowalczyk, Krzysztof Kuryłowicz, [the late] Janusz Magnuski, Paul Malmassari, Krzysztof Margasiński, Wawrzyniec Markowski, Mariusz Zimny, *Centralne Archiwum Wojskowe* (*Wojskowe Biuro Historyczne*) – Central Military Archives (Military Historical Bureau), *Archiwum Dokumentacji Mechanicznej* (*Narodowe Archiwum Cyfrowe*) – Archives of Mechanical Documentation (National Digital Archives), *Ośrodek "Karta"* – The "Karta" Centre, *Muzeum Wojska Polskiego* – Polish Army Museum, *Muzeum Historyczne w Legionowie* – Historical Museum in Legionowo, *Muzeum Niepołomickie* – Museum of Niepołomice.

Colour profiles: by the author – based on technical reconstruction drawings by Artur Przęczek, [the late] Witold Jeleń, [the late] Leszek Komuda and the author.

Special thanks to Mr. Artur Przęczek for creating and providing reconstructions of technical drawings of rolling stock, coaches, wagons and steam locomotives.

Translator's notes: the abbreviation P.P. – *pociąg pancerny* (armoured train) is applied throughout the book. The names of the individual armoured trains are retained in Polish. The abbreviation *wz.00 – wzór*" (issue / model) distinctively identifies any given piece of military equipment by the year of introduction.

INTRODUCTION

Armoured trains were extremely crucial weapon systems in the Polish-Ukrainian War of 1918–1919 and the Polish-Bolshevik War of 1919–1920. The dominating feature of both wars was manoeuvrability – hardly ever the battle-lines were truly defined. In mobile warfare with unstable fronts, combat trains were a formidable and effective weapon.

The exact number of armoured trains created in the period 1918–1921 cannot be established. There were several dozen of them – some operated for a very short time. The names, numbers and assignments changed, as well as the rolling stock composition. Some trains were assembled from whatever materials and armaments were at hand, and were described as armoured trains in a somewhat optimistic manner. Sometimes they did not even appear on the official weapon registries.

Depending on what criteria is applied, in total there were 85, maybe even 90 Polish combat trains. Those days and those trains require a special study – it is being prepared and will be released in the not too distant future. It will be the volume **"Polish Armoured Trains 1918–1921"**, in the same format and with the same narrative method as in this publication.

This volume begins in 1921 – after the war with Soviet Russia – and ends in September 1939 – the German invasion, followed 17 days later by the treacherous Soviet attack, thus starting a new Great War, this time designated as number "Two".

In a separate study, we plan to present armoured trains, undoubtedly Polish, but not belonging to the Polish Army. Such are the Polish trains of the I Corps formed in Russia in 1917, so when the Independent Republic of Poland had not yet existed, and the trains from Arkhangelsk and Novorossiysk, allied to the Entente, and formally belonging to the Polish Army in France, a separate Polish armed force combined with the Polish Army in the country only in September 1919.

"Polish-non-Polish" were also trains of the Central Lithuania army existing as a separate state from October 1920, after the so-called rebellion of *Generał* Lucjan Żeligowski, joined to the Polish in April 1922. The Army of Central Lithuania was an autonomous formation, under its own command.

The situation of Polish trains in the Wielkopolska Uprising was similar, although for different reasons. The Autonomous Greater Poland Army began to merge with the Polish Army in December 1919. Before that time, and after the victory of the uprising, the Greater Poland Army was operationally subordinate to the orders of the Polish Army, but inside it governed itself.

In Silesia, during the Third Uprising, the insurgent army was subordinate to the Supreme Command of the Insurgent Forces and only after the victory the Silesian armored trains formally became trains of the Polish Army, and the temporary I. Upper Silesian Armoured Train Regiment was disbanded only in 1923.

In September 1939, 10 regular armoured trains went into battle; a few improvised trains were created during the September Campaign.

To those who unwisely claim that armoured trains were wasted money and misused equipment assets, since even a single enemy aircraft could easily disable this obsolete weapon system... it is worth remembering, that these mobile four-gun artillery batteries – that is what in fact the armoured trains were – managed to inflict considerable losses to the enemy. It is also worth to emphasize that the P.P. 54 "*Groźny*" – the train with the shortest combat history – was not eliminated by the enemy, but only by a bridge that was prematurely blown up by retreating Polish troops. Armoured trains P.P. 53 "*Śmiały*", P.P. 55 "*Bartosz Głowacki*" and P.P. 51 "*Marszałek*" were in full working order after three weeks of defensive fighting. Armoured train P.P. 52 "*Piłsudczyk*" also remained in operation for three weeks and was intentionally derailed by the crew when the ammunition supply was exhausted. In the course of the campaign, in a single encounter, P.P. 53 "*Śmiały*" was able to demolish a large number of the German *Panzer Division* tanks during the battle of Mokra.

While it is true that anti-aircraft defences of the Polish armoured trains were inadequate, an addition of the modern "*Bofors*" 40 mm anti-aircraft gun allowed for a success in fending off enemy aerial assaults. Both, P.P. 51 "*Marszałek*" and P.P. 55 "*Bartosz Głowacki*" were supplemented by such guns during the campaign.

During the course of the 1939 defensive war, there was an enormous effort on part of the armoured train crews to dissolve huge railroad traffic jams. Many track repairs were very efficiently carried out – the training paid off.

So let us do justice to the heroic actions of the crews and pay tribute to the armoured trains of the Polish Army.

TABLE OF CONTENTS

BASE LOCATIONS

Tracks of Jabłonna railway station and a junction with a paved road from Warsaw to Zegrze and beyond... The building close to the railway crossing, below the tracks, is the mobilization warehouse of the 1. Dywizjon Pociągów Pancernych. The photograph was taken from an observation balloon around 1932.

Year 1921

After the end of the war with Soviet Russia at the end of November 1920, the Polish Army had 28 regular armoured. 24 trains were kept in active service; the rest became a mobilization reserve. They were organised into 12 groups (*dywizjon*) consisting of two trains each. In 1920 and 1921, no permanent locations were assigned – the trains were stationed in places from where they could most efficiently and easily join potential combat operations. Determining the whereabouts during this complex period of history is possible for some units only – locations were changing, and written accounts as well as surviving documents do not provide enough details.

There was a lot activity, exemplified by the armoured train "*Generał Iwaszkiewicz*". In November 1920, after the end of hostilities, the train was stationed in Chodorów, later, in December – while assigned to 2nd Army – it moved to Lwów, and then to Stanisławów. From January to mid-March 1921, it was again in Lwów, from where the train was dispatched to the *Dowództwo Generalne Okręgu Kraków* (General Command of District Cracow). In view of the German threat, in April the train was stationed in Skawina. In May, the Third Silesian Uprising broke out, and therefore an improvised train was assembled from some of the older combat wagons and sent to Upper Silesia with a volunteer crew. The equipment was incorporated into the insurgent P.P. 16 "*Ludyga*" armoured train. In mid-June 1921, "*Generał Iwaszkiewicz*" was sta-

tioned in Cracow, at the Bonarka railway station siding. From Bonarka it travelled to Jabłonna, where in September 1921 the crew was demobilised and the train was disbanded.

Another example is the P.P. 4 "*Hallerczyk*" armoured train. It was rearmed at the beginning of August 1920 in Jabłonna with new rolling stock of "warsaw" type wagons. The train fought in the eastern territories, and after the ceasefire, was stationed in Brześć (today Brest in Belarus). At the beginning of 1921, it was sent to Łuniniec to patrol the Łuniniec – Baranowicze railway route. In mid-April it was still at Łuniniec, but in the summer it was transferred to Stryj. In the late August 1921, P.P. 4 "*Hallerczyk*" was directed to Cracow, to the *1. Pułk Wojsk Kolejowych* (1st Railway Regiment), and disbanded.

By the end of 1921, the political situation was normalising – the units of railway engineers were leaving their wartime posts, and armoured trains were also arriving at the railway regiments in Poznań, Jabłonna and Cracow, according to their assignments.

Poznań-Górczyn

Armoured trains of the *3. Pułk Wojsk Kolejowych* (3rd Railway Troops Regiment) were stationed on the sidings at Górczyn station. It was a convenient location, with a very good rail connection with the entire Poznań railway hub, including two major railway workshops and the Cegielski Plant. As part of the thorough reorganization, in March 1924, armoured trains of the 3rd Regiment were distribut-

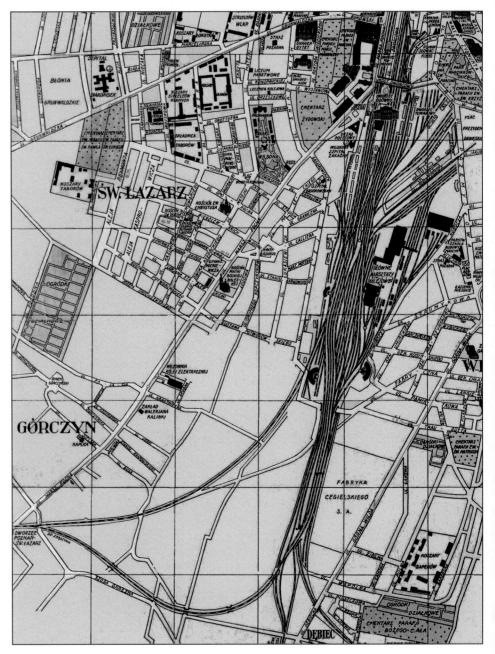

The track layout of the Poznań railway junction, in 1920's.

ed between the regiments in Jabłonna and Cracow in order to reform the units and scrap the useless equipment. In October 1924, the *3. Pułk Wojsk Kolejowych* was disbanded.

Jabłonna-Legionowo

The *Linia Kolei Nadwiślańskiej* (Line of Vistula Railway) was of great importance for the development of Jabłonna and the future Legionowo. The Jabłonna station was established in 1877, by 1892, a Tsarist garrison was established in the vicinity of the tracks. The railway route connected the most important Russian fortifications in Poland – the Dęblin Fortress, Warsaw and the Modlin Fortress. Jabłonna became one of the most important centres for the Russian troops. In 1915, after the Russians were ousted, the German troops occupied the barracks.

On 11 November 1918, a detachment of the volunteer underground forces *Polska Organizacja Wojskowa* (Polish Military Organisation) took over the Jabłonna station and warehouses in the garrison. And at the end of the month, the transformation of the volunteers into a regular

In the late 1920's – a characteristic view of Legionowo military depot. In the foreground, railway pioneers are practising an assembly a steel railway bridge of the Roth-Wagner system; in the background, on the left, the assault wagon Number 425627 of the P.P. 1 "Danuta" (before modifications).

The officers of the 1st Armoured Train Group (1. Dywizjon) by a log construction building, characteristic of the Legionowo barracks. Photograph from June 1931.

army began. In January 1919, the Infantry Inspectorate of Legions was established at the garrison in Jabłonna, and almost at the same time the military base was renamed Legionowo.

The parcelling out of the Jabłonna estate in 1925 designated the areas for the Jabłonna-Legionowo I zone, and in 1926 for the Jabłonna-Legionowo II zone.

At the base of Legionowo, a cadre of the *2. Pułk Wojsk Kolejowych* (2nd Railway Troops Regiment) was formed. The regiment was formally created in August 1921 after the return of the railway companies independently operating on the front lines. In 1924, as a result of reorganisation and transition to peace mode, the regiment changed its name to the

Commemorative badge of the 1. Dywizjon Pociągów Pancernych.

Legionowo – photo taken in 1928. Training grounds of the 2. Pułk Saperów Kolejowych (2nd Railway Pioneer Regiment), and later of the 2. Pułk Mostów Kolejowych (2nd Railway Bridge Battalion) and the 1. Dywizjon Pociągów Pancernych (1st Armoured Trains Group), and at the same time a field for balloon flights. On the left, partially obscured by the training bridge span, the balloon hangar of the 2. Batalion Balonowy (2nd Balloon Battalion) – this battalion was also stationed in Legionowo and shared the area with the "railroaders". On the right, a 600 mm narrow-gauge railway track of the bridge battalion with an RIIIc ex-Austrian steam locomotive. In the background an assault wagon of the "Danuta".

Opposite page: A photograph from the early 1930's (probably 1933) taken with the camera of the observation balloon of the 2. Batalion Balonowy. Jabłonna railway station – a view towards the Jabłonna estate. The "Polonia" air balloon is hovering over the tracks. The lower part of the image shows the area of the 1. Dywizjon. Interestingly, the concrete platform with frontal ramps exists to this day. On the left, just outside the frame, there was the building of the mobilization warehouse.

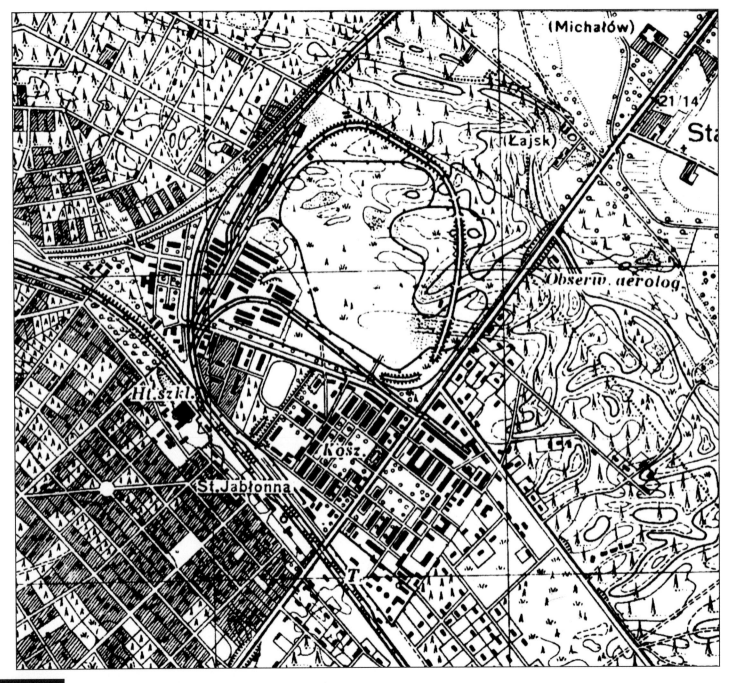

Legionowo on a map from the 1930's.

2. *Pułk Saperów Kolejowych* (2nd Railway Pioneer Regiment) – the armoured trains were still an integral part of the unit. In 1926, the construction of a military balloon base began as part of the area development. In 1927, the armoured trains were removed from under the command of the engineer regiment, consequently forming the 1. *Dywizjon Pociągów Pancernych* (1st Armoured Train Group).

In 1928, the zone of Jabłonna-Legionowo III was created, and in September, the 2. *Batalion Balonowy* (2nd Balloon Battalion) was formed at the Legionowo garrison. Since then, the Legionowo military base was occupied by three units: 1. *Dywizjon Pociągów Pancernych*, 2. *Pułk Saperów Kolejowych* – reformed in 1929 into the 2. *Batalion Mostów Kolejowych* (2nd Railway Bridge Battalion) – and 2. *Batalion Balonowy*. On 25 January 1934, the name of the Jabłonna military base was officially changed to Legionowo (the name of the railway station changed accordingly).

Non-commissioned officers of the emergency manoeuvre cadre train "Generał Sosnkowski", 1930's.

Left and right sides of the banner of the 1. Dywizjon Pociągów Pancernych.

Officers of the 1. Dywizjon Pociągów Pancernych, 1930's.

Niepołomice and Bonarka

The situation of the armoured trains stationed in Cracow was somewhat difficult. The staging tracks assigned to the *1. Pułk Wojsk Kolejowych* (1st Railway Troops Regiment) and its armoured trains did not have sufficient capacity so the trains had to be distributed between the various sidings. When the *2. Dywizjon Pociągów Pancernych* (2nd Armoured Train Group) was formed in the spring of 1928, Niepołomice became home to the group's headquarters, administrative platoon and an exercise train – the task carried out by armoured train *"Piłsudczyk"* at the time. Only with time the sidings were expanded and workshop facilities were built. At first the living conditions were difficult for the personnel – there were not enough quarters. Niepołomice was a tiny and poor town. It developed quite quickly, in part due to the presence of the armoured train

base, but it was not until 1939 when the town's population reached 5,000 inhabitants. Niepołomice was electrified (with a great effort on part of the unit's commander) only in 1935. Until then, energy for the base was supplied by a generator driven first by a steam locomotive, and later by a *Perkun* combustion engine. There were not enough water wells – new ones had to be dug out. Even as late as 1934, water was delivered in barrels, with a horse drawn cart.

Most of the *2. Dywizjon Pociągów Pancernych* rolling stock was stationed on the sidings of the Cracow-Bonarka railway station – a southern suburb of Cracow. The *"I. Marszałek"* was designated as an emergency manoeuvre armoured train, the rest was considered a mobilization reserve. The crew was housed in the barracks adjacent to the sidings. Additional warehouses were set up in makeshift sheds at the nearby Cracow-Płaszów railway station. Part of the rolling stock was also placed (especially in the 1920's) at the *Poligon Ćwiczebny* (Training Ground) of the *1. Pułk Saperów Kolejowych* (1st Railway Pioneer Regiment) – on the left bank of the Vistula River in the area near the Cracow-Grzegórzki railway station.

Commemorative badge of the 2. Dywizjon Pociągów Pancernych.

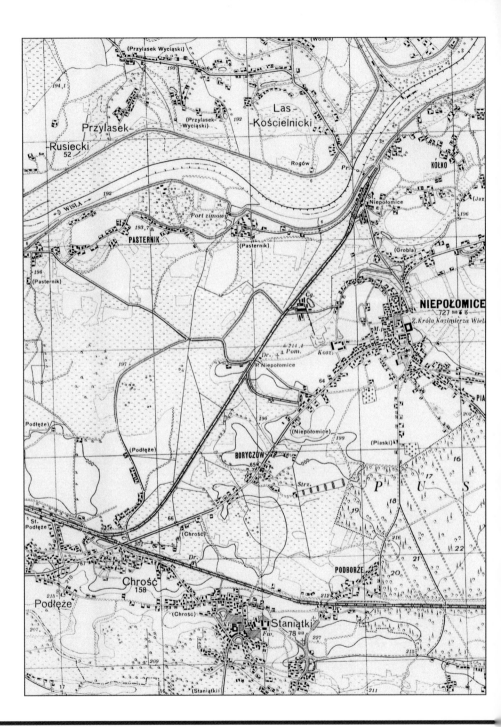

The Niepołomice town and the Podłęże junction station on the map from the 1930's.

A column of soldiers of the 2. Dywizjon Pociągów Pancernych *marching through the centre of Niepołomice, around 1937.*

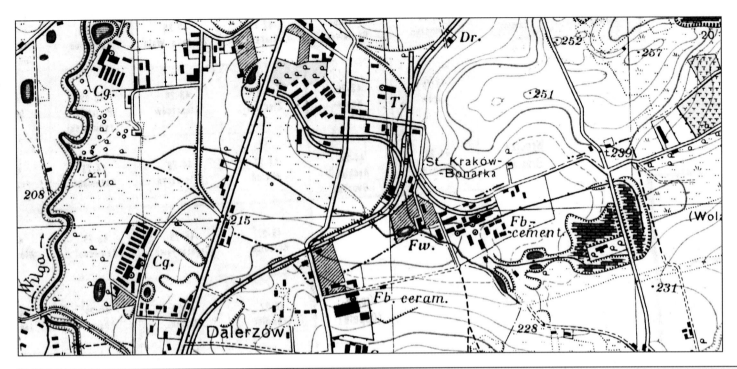

Bonarka on a map from the 1930's.

On the right: The officers of the 2. Dywizjon in the Market Square at Niepołomice, probably 1938.

A celebratory field mass on the occasion of the Armoured Train Groups' Day, Niepołomice in 1934.

KORPUS PODOFIC ZAWODOW 2 DYONU POCIĄG PANCER

5 CZERWCA 1937 R.

Training ground of the 1. Pułk Saperów Kolejowych next to the Kraków-Grzegórzki railway station. At the edge of the shed, the Ti3 armoured steam locomotive, and under the roof, the wagons of the "Groźny" armoured train may be seen. Photograph from 1927.

Opposite page: Tableau of active non-commissioned officers of the 2. Dywizjon – as of 5 June 1937, the Group's Day.

Images above: The Group's Day in 1937 – the NCO's table and, on the left, the visiting orchestra of the 20. Pułk Piechoty (20th Infantry Regiment), added the splendour to the ceremony. The 20. Pułk Piechoty trained and mobilized assault platoons for the trains P.P. 5 "Śmiały" and P.P. 6 "Groźny".

The football (soccer) team of a platoon of armoured draisines, 1934.

Opposite page photographs: The Group's Day in 1937 – the troops enjoying a meal at the tables.

Training grounds

The firing practice of the armoured trains, for both artillery and heavy machine guns, took place at the training ground in Rembertów near Warsaw, but also in swamps and quagmires near Czarny Dunajec, a small station on the line leading from Nowy Targ (build by Austro-Hungarian Empire and constructed to support heavy military trains and locomotives).

Artillery firing practices also took place at the training ground in the vicinity Dęblin.

Between 1935 and 1939, the crews of armoured trains participated in a gunnery training and tactical exercises in the eastern borderlands, near Pińsk (using the Parochońsk railway station as a base) or near Sarny. Training journeys were also performed to Czerwony Bór in Podlasie region.

A single-track line from Pilawa (Pilawa became the base of armoured trains during training) via Mińsk Mazowiecki to Tłuszcz was designated especially for the exercises of railway troops (mainly railway engineers). The *P.K.P.* excluded this line from commercial traffic to enable specialised exercises of track and infrastructure repair. The training was far more advanced than simple damaged rail replacement; it included construction of bridges, viaducts and culverts.

Soldiers of the 2. Dywizjon in Pilawa – note regulation, armoured troops overalls worn over the uniforms along with tank-type helmets (modified Adrian type).

The extensive track layout in Pilawa was perfect for armoured train exercises – officers of the 2. Dywizjon photographed in Pilawa during exercises in 1934.

The engine shed in Pilawa; exercises of armoured trains in 1934.

The Tatra draisine from the 2. Dywizjon in Pilawa, 1934.

The Szkoła Ognia (Firing School) – live firing practice with wz. 08 heavy machine guns (on field mounts) in Rembertów, 1938.

In both photographs, troops of the 1. Dywizjon Pociągów Pancernych during exercises in Czerwony Bór. On a side track, two TK-R-TK draisine sets covered with tarpaulins.

Photograph taken on 10 November 1933 in Tłuszcz near Warsaw. The ceremony to unveil the monument commemorating the fallen during the Battle for Warsaw. In the image, troops of the 1. Dywizjon Pociągów Pancernych (1st Armoured Train Group) may be seen. In the background, the "Danuta" sporting a new, experimental camouflage pattern, which survived a rather long time – until 1936.

ARMOURED TRAINS
1930–1939
1. DYWIZJON POCIĄGÓW PANCERNYCH
(1ˢᵗ ARMOURED TRAIN GROUP)

Previous page: Photograph taken on 10 November 1933 in Tłuszcz near Warsaw. The ceremony to unveil the monument commemorating the fallen during the Battle for Warsaw. In the image, troops of the 1. Dywizjon Pociągów Pancernych (1ˢᵗ Armoured Train Group) may be seen. In the background, the "Danuta" sporting a new, experimental camouflage pattern, which survived a rather long time – until 1936.

Next page: "Poznańczyk" armoured train. Front artillery wagon and locomotive, September 1939.

1. DYWIZJON POCIĄGÓW PANCERNYCH (1st ARMOURED TRAIN GROUP)

In December 1929 it was decided to disband the P.P. 12 "*Zagończyk*" (P.P. – *pociąg pancerny* – armoured train). At the same time, in 2nd Armoured Train Group stationed at Niepołomice the P.P. 8 "*Stefan Czarniecki*" train was decommissioned. The rolling stock acquired in this way was intended to replace or compliment the equipment of the remaining trains in both armoured train groups. The exchange of rolling stock and the new composition was left to the discretion of the unit commanders, but it had to be consulted with the headquarters of the respective parent units – the 1st and 2nd Battalion of Railway Bridges (*Batalion Mostów Kolejowych*).

On 10 January 1930 a final decision was approved to reconfigure the combat sections. The composition of the 1st Armoured Train Group was established as follows:

Armoured Train No. 1 "*Danuta*"
- artillery wagon 699049,
- artillery wagon 699050,
- assault wagon 620652

- armoured draisine.

Armoured Train No. 2 "*General Sosnkowski*"
- artillery wagon 699053,
- artillery wagon 699054,
- assault wagon 423502,
- armoured draisine.

Armoured Train No. 3 "*Paderewski*"
- artillery wagon 660601,
- artillery wagon 402634,
- assault wagon 425627,
- armoured draisine.

A photograph taken in 1931 at Jabłonna. The entire rolling stock seen in the image would be rebuilt and modernised in the 1930's. The Ti3-8 locomotive was eventually fitted with a compressor for brake installations accessible thru a two-panel inspection door in the boiler armour cover. The small artillery wagons would be rebuilt and transferred to Niepołomice, the assault wagon would have its turret removed and partially receive new armour, and of the last wagon, a part of which is seen on the right, only the gun turret and chassis will remain, while the armour of the casemate would be completely re-arranged.

Armoured Train No. 4 "Śmierć"
- artillery wagon 141164,
- artillery wagon 141455,
- assault wagon 390243,
- armoured draisine.

Armoured Train No. 11 "Poznańczyk"
- artillery wagon 699051,
- artillery wagon 699052,
- assault wagon 430044.

An artillery wagon 430047 remained with the 1st Armoured Train Group as a reserve. In fact, there were more armoured railcars left, including the single-turret artillery wagons of the old armoured train "Poznańczyk" from the era of the Polish-Soviet War, but under the new roster they became surplus.

The reassignment of the combat wagons between the Armoured Train Groups and between individual trains was quite extensive. A shortage of modern assault wagons became apparent, so a number of conversions were carried out – some of the artillery wagons were rebuild. The assault wagon 430044 in the new composition of the train No. 11 "Poznańczyk" was originally an artillery wagon from armoured train "Czarniecki" (previously armed with an Austrian 8 cm cannon). The same conversion was done to another wagon, also from "Czarniecki" – 423502; after removing the turret with its 8 cm gun, it became the assault wagon of the train No. 2 "Gen. Sosnkowski". The assault wagon of the train No. 4 "Śmierć" came from "Zagończyk". Unification of rolling stock was also carried out. The artillery wagon 699053, which was a part armoured train "Śmierć", was reassigned to train No. 3 "Gen. Sosnkowski" – so two identical wagons were paired in the

same train. The artillery wagons of the recomposed train No. 4 "Śmierć" came from "Zagończyk", again two identical artillery wagons were assigned to the same train. The short artillery wagons that served with "Bartosz Głowacki" train during the war with the Bolsheviks, and then were assigned to "Śmierć" and later to "Gen. Sosnkowski", were rebuilt and left

as reserve at Niepołomice – base of the 2nd Armoured Train Group. In 1939, they were used to form the training armoured detachment of the 2. Dywizjon. Minor assignment adjustments continued in the 1930s – for example, wagon 425627 from train No. 3 "Paderewski" was moved to train No. 1 "Danuta". It is difficult to precisely determine the fate of individual

wagons due to the voids in archival documentation. The challenge is compounded by the fact that some of wagons were re-numbered during reconstruction and repairs. For example, wagon 141455 from armoured train "Śmierć" received a new number – 153650 for no apparent reason; while the artillery wagons of "Paderewski" train after a thorough overhaul,

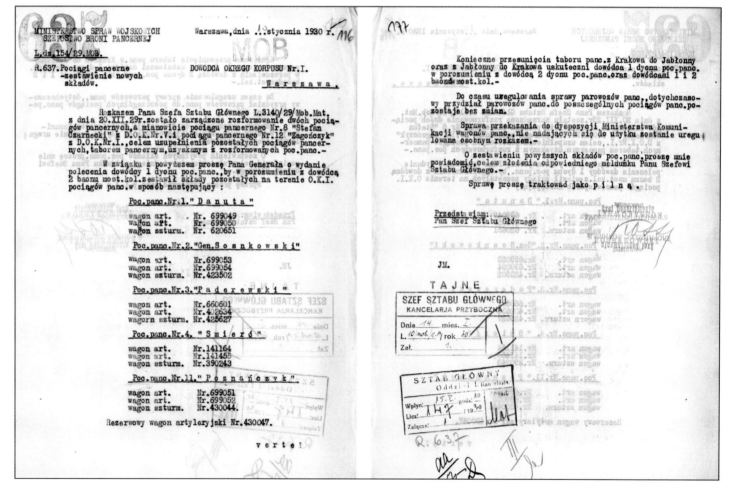

Order issued 10 January 1930 on the new composition of the 1. Dywizjon Pociągów Pancernych.

Załącznik Nr.1 do L.1053/Mob.Og.Mob.30
Dep.Uzbr.M.S.Wojsk.

Z E S T A W I N I E

działe, CKM., IKM. i amunicji do nich, potrzebnych na wyposażenie mob.pociągów pancernych
i dyonu poc.panc.według norm ustalonych do obecnego Planu mob.mat.uzbr.

NNr. poc. panc.	Części składowe poc.panc.	Jednostka mobilizu- jąca.	3" ap. res. wz.02 kompl.	10 cm. hb.as. wz.14 kompl.	8 cm. ap.as. wz.5/8	CKM nm. wz.08 kompl.	CKM. frs. wz.25 kompl.	IKM. nm. wz. 08/15 kempl	Gra- naty 3" res.	Szrap- nele 3" res.	Grana- ty 100mm. as.	Szrap- nele 100 mm. as.	Nb. 7,92mm. do K.M.	Nb. 7,92mm. do KBK.	U w a g i
Nr.1	D-ca poc.panc.z pocztem i druż.adm.,plutonami ogni- wemi NNr.I/1 i II/1 i drezyną panc.	1 dyon poc. panc.	2	2	-	20	2	-	240	360	300	100	660000	5840	
	Pluton techniczny	2 baon mest.kol.	2	2	-	2	2	-	-	-	-	-	-	1120	
	"" szturmowy	32 p.p.	-	-	-	-	-	2	-	-	-	-	60000	3000 1	1/ W zapasie mob 32 p.p.
Nr.2	D-ca poc.panc.w składzie jak d-ca popeNr.1	1 dyon mest. kol.	4	-	-	16	2	-	480	720	-	-	540000	5840	
	Pluton techniczny	2 baon mest.kol.	-	-	-	-	-	-	-	-	-	-	-	1120	
	"" szturmowy	30 p.p.	-	-	-	-	-	2	-	-	-	-	60000	3000 2	2/ W zap.mob. 30 p.p.
Nr.3	D-ca poc.panc.w składzie jak d-ca poc.panc.Nr.1	1 dyon poc. panc.	1	1	-	15	2	-	120	180	150	50	510000	5840	
	Pluton techniczny	2 baon mest. kol.	-	-	-	-	-	-	-	-	-	-	-	1120	
	"" szturmowy	21 p.p.	-	-	-	-	-	2	-	-	-	-	60000	3000 3	3/ W zap.mob. 21 p.p.
Nr.4	D-ca poc.panc.w składzie jak d-ca poc.panc.Nr.1	1 dyon poc. panc.	2	-	-	9	2	-	240	360	-	-	330000	5840	
	Pluton techniczny	2 baon mest. kol.	-	-	-	-	-	-	-	-	-	-	-	1120	
	"" szturmowy	36 p.p.	-	-	-	-	-	2	-	-	-	-	60000	3000 4	4/ W zap.mob. 36 p.p.
Nr.11	D-ca poc.panc.z pocztem i druż.admin.oraz plutonami ogniowemi NNr.I/11 i II/11	1 dyon poc.panc.	2	2	-	19	-	-	240	360	300	100	570000	5840	
	Pluton techniczny	2 baon mest. kol.	-	-	-	-	-	-	-	-	-	-	-	1120	
	"" szturmowy	18 p.p.	-	-	-	-	-	2	-	-	-	-	60000	3000 5	5/ W zap.mob. 18 p.p. /DOK Nr.IV/
Poc. panc. szkol.	Pociąg panc.szkolny	1 dyon poc. panc.	4	1	2	8	-	1	-	-	-	-	16500	2440	
	RAZEM:		15	6	2	82	8	11	1320	1980	750	250	2926500	52240	6/ gran.-szrapn. i szrapneli
	JEST:		15	6	2	76	8	23	1800	2700 6	-	-	3280000	52240	
	BRAK:		-	-	-	11	-	-	-	-	750	250	-	-	
	NADWYŻKA:		-	-	-	-	-	12	480	720	-	-	353500	-	

Appendix to a mobilisation table from 1930.

and than a subsequent one, were given the final numbers 658641 and 660588 as their armoured structure was transferred to the new carriages (the final numbering scheme was based on the *P.K.P. – Polskie Koleje Państwowe* [Polish National Railways] system, where the first three digits identified the type and characteristics of the wagon).

The assignment of the *Tatra* draisines was also changed. Out of the three draisines in the 2nd Armoured Train Group, two remained, while the third was transferred to the 1st Group at Legionowo. With four *Tatra* draisines available, they were assigned to armoured train No. 1 "*Danuta*", No. 2 "*Gen. Sosnkowski*", No. 3 "*Paderewski*" and No. 4 "*Śmierć*".

At the same time, unification of steam locomotives was slowly progressing. Series *Ti3* (ex Prussian *G5.³* slated as a standard armoured engines) were replacing the variety of the older ones, in both Armoured Train Groups. The un-armoured *Ti3* engines were also declared to be standard equipment of the Battalions of Railway Bridges. In May 1931, *Ti3-3*, *Ti3-5*, *Ti3-8* and *Ti3-12* were at the disposal of the *1. Dywizjon Pociągów Pancernych*. At that time, the unit still had the *Ti1-26* locomotive (formerly Prussian *G5.¹* 4018) and the *Tp1-112* locomotive (formerly Prussian *G7* series). Some time later, a fifth armoured locomotive *Ti3* with the number 16 and the "black", un-armoured, *Ti3-14* were delivered to the 1st Armoured Train Group (the *Ti3-14* was swapped with the *Ti3-6* locomotive from Krakow-Bonarka base of the 2nd Armoured Train Group).

In the 1930's some major as well as minor changes were introduced to the com-bat wagons of Polish armoured trains. One of the most significant modifications, carried out in both groups, was the replacement of artillery pieces (the process began in the late 1920s). The Russian 3-inch guns (76.2 mm) *wz. 02* (model 1902) and anti-aircraft guns *wz.14*, were substituted with a re-bored version designated as the *wz. 02/26*. These modified guns were adapted to fire ammunition of French design, calibre 75 mm – the same as used in Polish field artillery guns, *Schneider wz. 1897*. The installation of the guns did not present a problem, as the existing gun mounts could be kept without any modifications since the trunnions did not change in any way. Due to the introduction of different ammunition, a new scale on the aim sights, French type fuse keys, as well as new firing tables were provided.

The Russian 122 mm *wz. 09* guns were also abandoned, as in the rest of the army, in favour of the 100 mm *Škoda wz. 14/19* howitzers. The demand for the 122 mm calibre ammunition was low, so maintaining its production for a dozen or so howitzers – there were only a few of them in armoured trains plus a dozen more in the entire ground forces – was completely pointless.

Machine guns were not changed – the heavy, jam prone, and complicated to operate, German-built *Maxim wz. 08* machine guns performed adequately in the trains. Their large weight did not matter as they were stationary, and the chance of getting mud or dust jamming them was much smaller than in the field.

On the other hand, the light *Maxim wz. 08/15* machine guns that equipped assault wagons and the sortie platoons were exchanged for a standard *wz. 28 Browning LMG's*.

Other major modifications included the modernisation of command posts located on the locomotive tenders. More importantly, the installation of a standardized machine gun turrets for anti-aircraft defence on artillery wagons (the process was started in the late 1920s) was carried out.

New equipment was also added, for example the installation of wireless communication sets in assault wagons (experimented with since 1926 on the train "*Danuta*"), and installation of *RKB/c* radio stations for communication with the

A cropped and enlarged part of a photograph from Jabłonna, taken in approximately 1935. As may be seen, artillery wagon from the old "Poznańczyk" was retained. We do not know however, if it was a part of the mobilisation reserve or a kind of remnant of the past.

A "Danuta" assault wagon in front of the workshop building in Jabłonna during refurbishment.

R and TK draisines. Towards the end of the 1930s, the installation of emplacements in the command posts on the tenders had begun in order to arm them with the wz. 28 light machine guns.

Part of all this work was performed by specialised railway and military workshops, while other, less complicated tasks, were carried out at the bases of the Armoured Train Groups. The unit's workshops were well equipped and employed qualified military as well as civilian professionals. As a side note, the 1st Armoured Train Group was also entrusted with the repair and maintenance of the Castle Column (Kolumna Zamkowa) vehicles, which were used by the President and the other important state officials. The workshops manufactured and fitted fans that ventilated out the gun powder fumes in the combat wagons. Stowage compartments for tools and materials for track repairs in the under-frames were also added to some of the Pdks series control flat railcars. Much more technically challenging tasks were also undertaken. Two experimental flat railcars with small wheel sets and offloading ramps were constructed to carry scout tankettes before the introduction of alternative solution – a standard rail guide frames for transporting the TKS tankettes. There was no follow up since the guide frame proved itself to be much better. Even more significantly, the unit's workshops build the first prototype of a rail undercarriage for the Renault FT tank. Among other achievements, a prototype anti aircraft mount for the heavy machine gun was designed and built. It was intended to equip the typical Kd series covered goods wagons with a brakeman's cab used in train support echelons.

In 1939, as part of the transition of the unit organisation to the wartime system, new names (in fact, codenames) were given to the armoured trains, and the train compositions were arranged according to the rosters. The name change was carried out according to a fairly simple key applied to the names of all units mobilised by the Polish Army – the P.P. was the abbreviation of pociąg pancerny; the first digit – signified the number of the Corps District (Okręg Korpusu – in the case of the 1. Dywizjon – District I, Warsaw); the second digit – train number in the consecutive order of mobilisation.

The presentation of the trains on the following pages has been arranged according to the mobilisation numbering from 1939. The descriptions of the rolling stock are focused on the most important period – 1939. The colour profiles of the wagons and steam locomotives depict the appearance and camouflage of the rolling stock in 1939.

The early 1930's in Jabłonna – artillery wagon 699054 of the "Generał Sosnkowski" on the terminus track at the unit's workshop.

Armoured Train No. 11
(P.P. 1 "Danuta")

Armoured Train No. 11 (P.P. 11 "Da-nuta") was mobilised in the last days of August 1939 using the equipment of the peacetime train P.P. No. 1 "Danuta".

P.P. 1 "Danuta" photographed in July 1935.

Opposite page and upper photograph: May 1935, the crew of "Danuta" during a briefing before departure from Legionowo as the Guard of Honour for a train carrying the coffin of Marshal Piłsudski to Cracow.

On the right: "Danuta" as the Guard of Honour somewhere between Warsaw and Cracow.

Next page: "Danuta" in an image taken in July 1935.

Conscripts being sworn into the 1. Dywizjon by the armoured train "Danuta" (Ti3-5 locomotive, from the regular composition of "Śmierć", before modernisation), 1933.

Funeral train with the coffin of Marshal Piłsudski entering the railway station in Cracow. On the neighbouring track, the front artillery wagon in this particular line-up of the armoured train.

Funeral train with the coffin of Marshal Piłsudski entering the railway station in Cracow – on the right a rear artillery wagon of "Danuta".

Another image of Marshal Piłsudski's funeral in Cracow – on the right a front artillery wagon.

Locomotive

The *Ti3* locomotive number 12 (former Prussian Railways *G5.³* number 4021, from the Hohenzollern factory, built in 1905) with the *12C1* tender Number 480 was used in the combat section of the P.P. 1 "*Danuta*", that is in September 1939 the P.P. 11. It was one of two *G5.³* locomotives that were initially armoured in the 1920s; it was used in the armoured train "*Mściciel*" – favourable opinions about this locomotive and its armour influenced the decision to adopt *Ti3* locomotives as standard locomotives for armoured trains.

The Ti3-12 with a 12C1-480 tender assigned to "Danuta" as a regulation locomotive (still before modification of inspection doors and hatches of the chassis armour).

A profile of the Ti3-12 locomotive with tender number 480.

Locomotive of the "Danuta" – Ti3-12 with 12C1-480 tender.

Artillery Wagons

Two identical artillery wagons with the numbers 699049 and 690950 were used. These were the so-called "Type II" wagons constructed on German four axle flat railcar chassis, assigned "*Danuta*" armoured train since January 1930.

During their years of service, the chassis of the wagons were modernised, as Westinghouse brake systems were installed. The continuous armoured sheet – an apron covering the undercarriage (with a round covers allowing access to the axle bearings) was changed at the end of the 1930s. Only the sections that covered the wheel bogies and the air brake installation were left. The armament consisted of a 75 mm *wz. 02/26* gun and a 100 mm *wz. 14/19A* howitzer, replacing the previous guns – the Russian 76.2 mm *wz.02* gun and 122 mm *wz. 09* howitzer. Both artillery pieces were mounted in rotating turrets. The armament was supplemented by eight *wz. 08* heavy machine guns in embrasures in the side walls of the wagon (the drum mounts of the weapons were at on point slightly modified so that the axis of the drum was vertical) and a heavy machine gun in the turret capable of anti-aircraft defence.

A commemorative photograph of the unit's non-commissioned officer's academy with the commanding cadre seen against an artillery wagon of "Danuta" in 1934.

The "Danuta" artillery wagon, in September 1939, used as the front wagon.

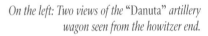

On the left: Two views of the "Danuta" artillery wagon seen from the howitzer end.

Opposite page: Troops of the signals platoon of the 1. Dywizjon photographed against the "Danuta" artillery wagon.

A profile of the rear wagon as of September 1939.

On the left:
Rear of the artillery wagon seen from a gun-turret's side.

Photograph taken inside the artillery wagon – a machine gun mount under the howitzer turret.

In the background, the assault wagon of "Danuta".

Assault Wagon

According to original plans, it was supposed to be the 620651 wagon, but the modifications were necessary, so "*Danuta*" received a wagon which was numbered 425627 according to the records of *P.K.P.* roster. Wagon 620651 was eventually assigned to the armoured train "*Poznańczyk*".

The wagon was built on the chassis of a Prussian two-axle (originally with a brakeman's cab) coal railcar with a capacity of 20 tons. In the interwar period, the armour layout underwent a thorough modification, which resulted in a change of the armour plate arrangement. The sections were joined by welding, and the only rivets and bolts were used to fix the plates to the framework of the railcar.

Some of the most important modifications included the removal of the brakeman's cab and the extension of the side armour to cover the brake platform. The observation turret on the top was removed, and the heavy machine gun ports were modernised by installing typical drum mounts. The grease-box cover plates were replaced with a sheet of armour protecting the chassis elements along the entire length of the wagon. Additional modernisations consisted of installing a wireless set compartment in the middle part of the interior and an antenna on the top of the wagon.

In the 1930s, the wagon underwent another, final modification, consisting of cutting out parts of the continuous chassis armoured cover.

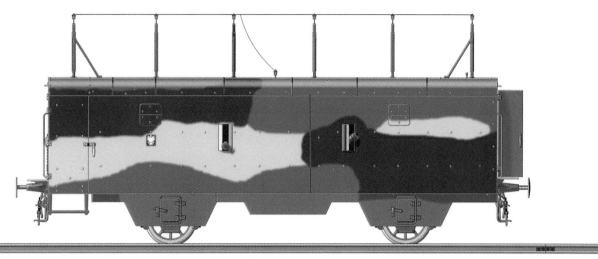

Assault wagon 425627.

The "Danuta" assault wagon. The inscription – 425621 – written with chalk is erroneous, probably a result of a mistake. The photograph was most likely taken in 1935, but the wagon is still in the 1933 camouflage pattern. The armour plates protecting the chassis were not modified yet, either.

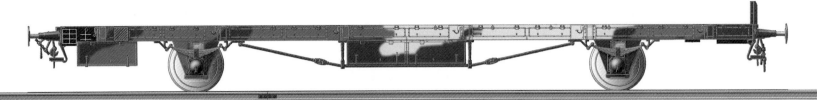

A profile of Pdks flat railcar of the "Danuta" with stowage boxes under the frame.

A profile of the TK-R-TK draisine set of the "Danuta"
(it was abandoned on the railway crossing at the village of Zduny).

Combat Flat Railcars

The front flat railcar of P.P. 11 was a standardized combat version of the wagon of the *Pdks* series, (Polish type *C-VIII*) with compartments and equipment stowage boxes in the under-frame.

Wheelbase of 8 m, nominal loading length 13 m (in fact 13.1 m), overall length 14.4 m and the load capacity 17.5 t were the characteristics of this type of the railcar.

The second flat railcar, the rear one, was also of the *Pdks* series, but it was an ordinary platform, not rebuilt and not camouflaged (left in its usual civilian red-brown), delivered by the *P.K.P.*

Draisine Platoon

Two sets of *TK-R-TK* reconnaissance rail vehicles (*Renault FT* tanks and *TKS* tankettes) were assigned to the train No. 11. A spare *TKS* tankette was carried in the support train section.

Administrative Supply Train Section

Most likely, as the echelon was formed during peacetime, the composition was in par with the regulations.

A German aerial photograph of the "Danuta" abandoned by its crew. The fire in the artillery wagon had clearly extinguished itself, only the tender is smouldering due to the coal fire.

"Danuta" in September 1939

Armoured Train No. 11 (P.P. 11), under the command of Captain Bolesław Korobowicz, was assigned to support the 26. *Dywizja Piechoty* (26th Infantry Division), and on 27 August 1939 entered the area of operations.

The day the war broke out, on 1 September 1939, the train set off from the Margonin station to patrol the Chodzież-Szamocin line; the next day it was patrolling the Kcynia-Nakło route, as a cover for the right flank of the 26th Division.

On 3 September, near Kcynia, it covered the withdrawal of subunits of the 26th Division to the Żnińskie Lakes line. On 4 September, in Szubin, the train was attacked by German aircraft, but without success. In the evening of that day, the train was directed to the Białe Błota station near Bydgoszcz, to the sector of the 15th Division of the Armia "Pomorze" (Pomeranian Army), and provided artillery support from the forest near the Wilczak bridgehead aimed at the German forces in the Czyżkówka area.

On the night of September 5-6, the train approached the Bydgoszcz Canal, where it was shelled by German anti-tank guns. Withdrawn to Kcynia, it left for Rąbinek just outside Inowrocław (it was briefly in the Operational Group of General Drapella covering the withdrawal of Polish troops from the Toruń region). The support echelon was held up in Szubin due to the track blockage so the combat section lost contact with it. The situation soon led to the shortage of ammunition and supplies.

In the evening of 7 September P.P. 11 left Rąbinek and on 9 September, it arrived at the Kutno station via Kłodawa. Two armoured trains were at this point gathered at Kutno – the P.P. 14 was already there. Both trains were subordinated to the Operational Group of General Bołtuć.

On 11 September P.P. 11 was directed to the area of Sochaczew – since the arrival of German armour units was expected there. The train managed to reach the Żychlin station without any problems, but it was halted by extensive damage to the tracks in the area. Over the next two days, in order to enable further travel, the train crew laid new tracks in place of the damaged ones, and even had to rebuild a large part of the embankment.

In the morning of 13 September, the train reached the Jackowice station. A platoon of the train's *TK* tankettes was sent out for reconnaissance – it came under German fire. One of the tankettes was damaged, but an impromptu repair was successful and the platoon returned to the train with no losses.

On 15 September, the P.P. 11 crew found four 75 mm field guns with an ammunition supply in an abandoned evacuation train. They were used to create a provisional battery between Zduny and Sobota, which together with the train's guns contributed to repelling German attacks near Bogiał. In the afternoon of that day, the train was assigned to the 16th Division –it stopped German movements on the right flank of the Division with well aimed artillery fire.

On 16 September the train repelled the German attack near Jackowice. However, the fire of German anti-tank guns immobilised the train, killing the crew of the locomotive. In addition one of the gun turrets sustained a hit. At this time, the

In both images, the burning artillery wagon of the "Danuta", 16 September 1939.

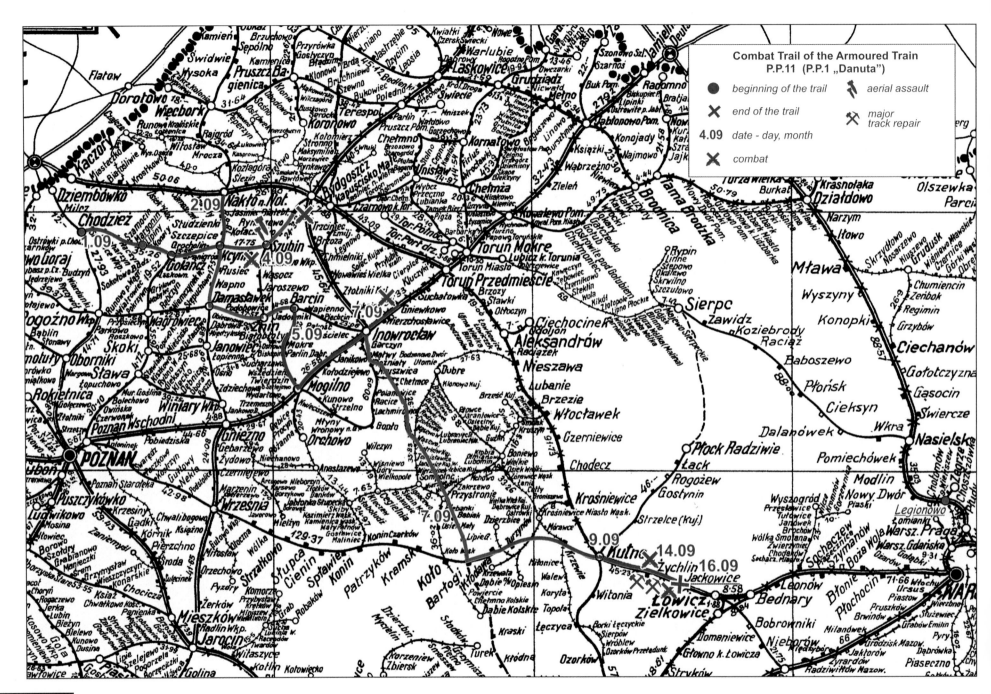

"Danuta" abandoned by its crew – in the upper picture the front wagon and tender are not burning any more.

On the right: The fire in the artillery wagon had died down, but coal in the tender is still burning.

Opposite page: Combat route of the P.P. 11 armoured train.

"Danuta" and its burnt out front wagon. The train had been pushed to a different location.

Many German troops passing nearby examined "Danuta" with great curiosity.

The rear artillery wagon and a part of the assault wagon. It can clearly be seen that the rear flat railcar is of regular Pdks type, with no storage boxes.

Opposite page: Troops of various German units (including cyclists) at the rear artillery wagon.

Assault wagon and the rear artillery wagon of the "Danuta".

A German soldier at the howitzer-turret of the rear wagon.

The rear artillery wagon. It is not known whether the wooden stairway was a part of the train's equipment.

Assault wagon and the rear artillery wagon.

The "Danuta" locomotive with clearly visible identification plates. This photograph was taken shortly after the train had been captured –the plate with the White Eagle was already taken away as a souvenir.

ammunition ran out (losing contact with the support section train took effect). Captain Korobowicz ordered the train to be sabotaged and abandoned.

The crew of the train marched towards the lower Bzura River and on 18 September joined the divisional cavalry of the 4th Division. On the next day, most were taken prisoner by the Germans. A few of the soldiers reached Warsaw, where they joined the crew of one of the improvised armoured trains formed for the defence of the capitol.

The locomotive was not heavily damaged and after being dis-armoured it was used by the Germans. It is on the list of operational Ostbahn (Eastern Railway) steam locomotives for 1940, with the note that it remained in the service of the Wehrmacht. The artillery wagons, severely damaged, were unsuitable for reconstruction and use. The assault wagon was repaired and after some time used by the Germans in the *Panzerzug Pz. 21* armoured train.

Regular excursions of German troops to examine the train were never-ending – here troops at the burnt out front wagon.

To the right: The rear wagon of the "Danuta" had been towed to a temporary depot of captured equipment.

The rear artillery wagon of the "Danuta", and in the background P.P. 52 "Piłsudczyk" wagons in a depot of war spoils.

The howitzer turret, of the "Danuta" rear artillery wagon in a depot.

Both images depict an R draisine abandoned near the village of Zduny. The fate of the tankettes which managed to leave the rail guide remains unknown. There were some hypotheses but none are truly convincing.

An R draisine with both TK rail guides, it seems that the rear one was be towed away (see previous page) earlier than the rest.

Armoured Train No. 12
(P.P. 11 "Poznańczyk")

The P.P. 11 *"Poznańczyk"* was mobilised under the codename Armoured Train No. 12 (P.P. 12).

Towards the very end of 1930's, P.P. 12 "Poznańczyk" was more often used as an exercise train (earlier, for instance in 1933 and 1934, this role was carried out by the "Generał Sosnkowski"). In 1935-37, it was "Danuta" which was used most often.

A commemorative photo taken in March 1937 of the "Poznańczyk" (the locomotive is "borrowed" – it was the regular engine of the "Paderewski").

"Poznańczyk" during exercises, most likely in 1938.

"Poznańczyk" during exercises – a photograph probably taken in 1937.

Ti3-16 locomotive seen from the front.

The "Poznańczyk" artillery wagon – an edge of the assault wagon is noticeable on the right.

The howitzer-armed turret of the "Poznańczyk". Image taken in July 1938 during exercises in Dąbrowica.

Profile of the Ti3-16 locomotive with 16D1-201 tender.

Locomotive

The P.P.12 train used a *Ti3* locomotive with the number 16 (former Prussian Railways, Number 4118, built in 1904 at the Humbolt factory) coupled with the only four-axle *16D1* tender (number 201) used by the armoured locomotives. A characteristic feature of locomotive number 16, which made it easy to identify, was a metal pennant in front of the funnel – none of the others had such a peculiarity. It is not known when a four-axle tender was coupled to this locomotive – a photograph taken in the second half of the 1930's shows the engine with a three-axle tender (in September 1939 this three-axle tender was used with the *Ti3-3* locomotive in the P.P. 13 train).

The "Poznańczyk" rolling stock with a prototype diesel-electric locomotive.

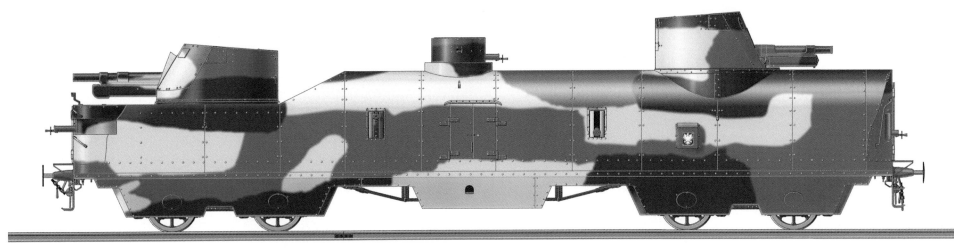

Side view of the artillery wagon (in September 1939 it served as the front artillery wagon).

Artillery Wagons

The artillery wagons of the P.P. 12 train, identical to the artillery wagons of the P.P. 11 ("*Danuta*") were manufactured by the Cegielski Factory in Poznań, as part of the "Type II" series. The base wagons had the numbers 699051 and 699052. Conversions and modifications were carried out in a manner similar to the "*Danuta*" train.

Assault Wagon

Initially this was supposed to be the assault wagon number 430044, but in the end an assault wagon 620651 was used. This wagon was one of several artillery and assault wagons known as "warsaw type", constructed at the beginning of 1920 on the chassis of Russian flat rail-

cars (1,000 – pood cargo capacity, wheel-base 5.5 m, frame length 9.2 m). An unquestionable curiosity was that the floor of the these armoured flat railcars had no protection, it remained wooden. In 1939, the *1. Dywizjon* asked for permission to replace or reinforce 620651's floor boards with steel plates, but it is not known whether this was carried out. The wagons of this type had a characteristic arched roof. The rifle ports were made with the use of ex-Austrian trench shields. During the interwar service, twin doors were installed in the sides of the wagon (previously wagons had doors only in the end walls), the observation turret on the roof was removed, the machine gun emplacements were rebuilt and a wireless communication equipment with the antenna posts was installed. The earliest, experimental, version of the antenna had two angular masts with a T-shaped crossbar.

Rear wall of the artillery wagon (seen from the cannon-armed turret side).

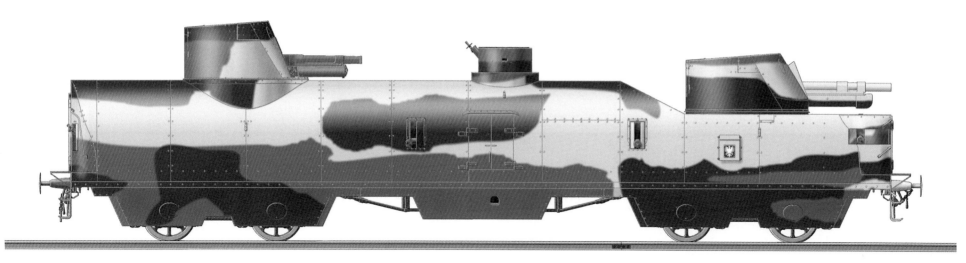

The second artillery wagon of the "Poznańczyk".

Combat Flat Railcars

Front and rear flat railcars of the P.P. 12 were of standard "combat" design – *Pdks* series, Polish type *C-VIII*. Both flat railcars, unlike other trains which had rear flat cars delivered by *P.K.P.*, were the unit's own platform railcars, equipped with compartments and equipment stowage boxes in the under-frame. Noteworthy, prior to the introduction of the "combat" *C-VIII* flat railcars, the trains were equipped with American-built four-axle flat railcars used during exercises.

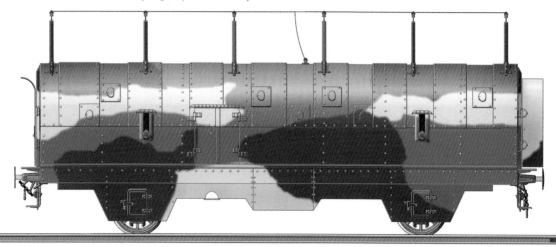

Assault wagon 620651.

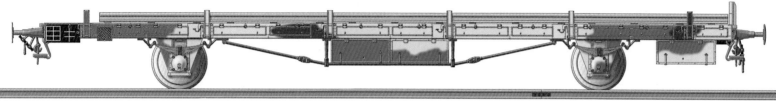

A Pdks flat railcar of the "Poznańczyk" with stowage boxes under the frame – in September 1939, it was used as the rear flat railcar. The front flat railcar was also equipped with stowage boxes.

Draisine platoon and "Poznańczyk" on a special mission as the Armoured Train No. 260, codenamed "Syrena", in the autumn of 1938. It supported the re-claiming of the Zaolzie area – the Czech part of Cieszyn Silesia.

Draisine Platoon

Two *TK-R-TK* half-platoons each with one *Renault FT* tank and two *TKS* tankettes, as well as an additional *TKS* tankette (including a spare rail guide frame) were a part of the train.

Administrative Supply Train Section

Probably in par with the established standards – lack of precise information.

"Poznańczyk" in September 1939

The P.P. 12 train entered its planned area of operations prior to the outbreak of the war, and on 31 of August 1939 it was assigned to cooperate with the *56. Pułk Piechoty* (56th Infantry Regiment of the 25th Division), which assumed the defensive positions on the approaches to Krotoszyn. On the morning of 1 September the train left Krotoszyn station towards Krotoszyn Stary and fired on German infantry near Cieszków (Freyhan), discharging 80 rounds and contributing significantly to repelling the enemy. Then, the train patrolled the railway line from Krotoszyn to Rawicz and supported Polish troops in the fighting for that town. In the evening of the same day, between Bażęcin and Wolenice, P.P. 12 covered the withdrawal of the Polish infantry towards Prosna. The draisines were sent off for reconnaissance in the direction of the frontier.

On 2 September the P.P. 12 travelled to Jarocin, where it was assigned to the *Wielkopolska Brygada Kawalerii* (Greater Poland Cavalry Brigade), patrolling the lines to Krotoszyn and Gostyń. On 3 September the train monitored the approaches to the bridges on the Warta River near Nowe Miasto.

The next day, 4 September, the train was carrying out reconnaissance towards Jarocin, making contact with the enemy in the evening. By order of the Brigade, it was directed to Warsaw – the movement of the combat and supply train sections through Września was very difficult due to extensive damage and blockage of the tracks by trains knocked-out by enemy bombardment. Along the way the train was also attacked by German aircraft. It was only on 6 September that it reached Kutno, but on the next day it was immobilised near Warsaw in a huge jam stretching from Błonie to Sochaczew.

The R and TK draisines of the "Poznańczyk".

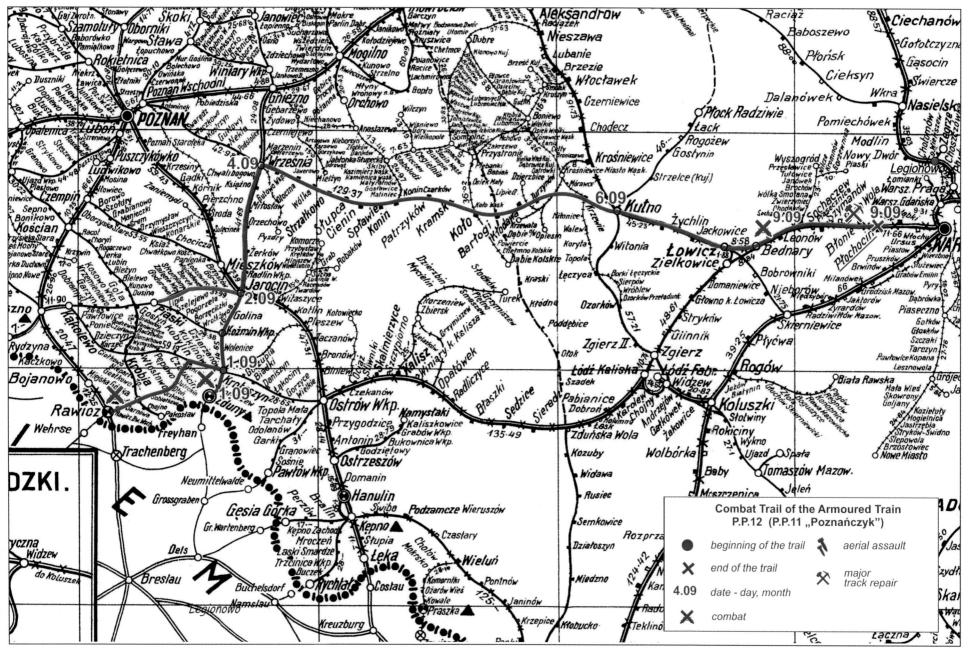

Combat route of the "Poznańczyk" in September 1939.

**Combat Trail of the Armoured Train
P.P.12 (P.P.11 „Poznańczyk")**

●	beginning of the trail	⚒	aerial assault
✕	end of the trail	⚒	major track repair
4.09	date - day, month		
✕	combat		

"Poznańczyk" *seen in a relatively early photograph – damage is visible; the flat railcars and the draisines were not towed away yet (September 1939).*

In the morning of 9 September there was a serious engagement with German forces aiming to take control of the Bzura River crossings. The fire from the train stopped the German troops near Leonowo, but the artillery brought up by the enemy forced P.P. 12 to retreat to Błonie. The train eventually departed from Błonie towards Warsaw. The Germans had already taken Ołtarzew –seeing no chance of breaking through to the state's capital, the train commanding officer, Captain K. Majewski, ordered the train to be incapacitated and abandoned at the Płochocin station,. The crew marched off by various routes to Warsaw, where they were incorporated into the bridge protection battalion.

The destruction of the train was extremely effective – none of the armoured wagons could be rebuilt, all were scrapped by the Germans. There is an unsolved mystery – the earliest photographs taken just after the train had been captured by the German troops show the equipment in a clearly better condition than in the later images. It is not known whether the delayed action explosives were rigged on the train, or whether the damages were inflicted by the Germans before the wreckage was pushed off the track.

The locomotive was an exception, it was later used by the Germans – it is listed on the roster as being in service with the *Wehrmacht*. The flat railcars remained undamaged as well.

In both photographs, the rear artillery wagon can be seen, as well as an assault wagon and locomotive, Płochocin station, September 1939.

Damage to the rear part of the train.

In this image, we can see a part of the flat railcar and the front artillery wagon.

Locomotive and the front artillery car. Below, the same equipment seen from the opposite side of the train.

Once the wagons had been pushed off the track, the locomotive was prepared to travel under its own steam. In the photographs below, the same locomotive is seen still between the wagons.

The "Poznańczyk" locomotive at the station in Sochaczew.

Locomotive of the "Poznańczyk" in Sochaczew. Note a part of a flat railcar equipped with stowage boxes seen on the right.

"Poznańczyk" wagons derailed and pushed off the embankment.

The photographs on this page depict the front artillery wagon after it had been derailed.

Opposite page, upper image: A turret armed with a howitzer of the front wagon.

Below and next: The assault car – the picture of the interior demonstrates that the internal explosion completely tore out the floor of the wagon.

In the upper and left photographs, a half-platoon of draisines which was closest to the "Poznańczyk" at the time it was abandoned.

View of the rear part of the draisine set – tankettes still with their armament and the second track occupied by another train – hence the conclusion that this image was taken relatively soon after the equipment had been captured.

The "Poznańczyk" set of draisines photographed still at Płochocin, but the neighbouring track has been unblocked and the tankettes have their guns removed.

An R draisine, an empty rail guide and a TK draisine. The front end of the Ti3 locomotive which pulled the evacuation train of the Batalion Mostów Kolejowych (Railway Bridge Battalion).

The draisine set, flat railcar and locomotive of the "Poznańczyk" after being towed to a siding track of the Sochaczew station.

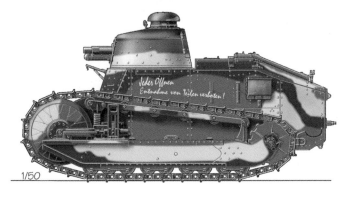

A Renault FT-17 *tank of the "Poznańczyk" armoured draisine R.*

The Germans considered the tank seized from the "Poznańczyk" armoured train as part of the Wehrmacht propaganda machine, and presented it in various locations in the area of Sochaczew and Łowicz.

Armoured Train No. 13
(P.P. 2 "Generał Sosnkowski")

In the last days of August 1939, P.P. 2 "*Generał Sosnkowski*" was mobilised in Legionowo, and was attached to the *Armia "Modlin"* as P.P. 13.

Locomotive

Armoured train "*Generał Sosnkowski*" was assigned a locomotive with the number *Ti3-3* (former Prussian number 4125, produced by Hanomag in 1904), with the *12C1* tender numbered 483. The armour of this particular locomotive had been arranged in a slightly different manner than on the other ones. The armour consisted of only five segments. Each of the arched profile sheets extended from the right to the left apron without any horizontal joints. Initially, there were four inspection hatches with horizontal hinges in each of the side aprons protecting the chassis of the steam locomotive. In the 1930's, the hatches were replaced with inspection doors.

The roster locomotive Ti3-3 of the "Generał Sosnkowski", in approximately 1936. In those days, it was coupled with a four-axle 16C1-201 tender. The tender already has the antenna posts fitted, while the locomotive is awaiting modification of the armour plates protecting the chassis as well as a coat of paint to conform to the new camouflage pattern.

"Generał Sosnkowski" – year 1937. The rolling stock in process of repainting according to the new pattern, flat railcars with stowage compartments and the new camouflage pattern. The locomotive was "the Eight" – Ti3-8, formally assigned to "Paderewski".

A profiles of the same Ti3-3 locomotive with the three-axle 12C1-483 tender.

Artillery Wagons

The combat section of the P.P. 13 included two nearly identical artillery wagons with the numbers 699053 and 699054. These wagons were built in 1920 and were the first twin turret armoured wagons on a four-axle chassis constructed in Poland. They were built at *HCP* (Cegielski Factory) in Poznań – they were referred to as "Type I". Initially, there were supposed to be an entire series of such wagons to equip at least four trains. But August 1920 brought the victory in the Polish – Soviet war; therefore, there was no longer a need for any new armoured trains. The Prussian flat railcars with a frame length of 13 m and a bogie wheel base of 8 m were used as the

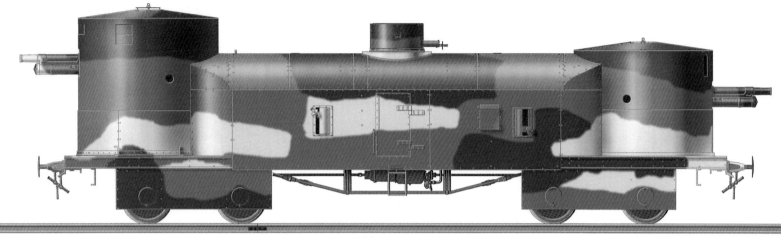

Side view of the artillery wagon 699053.

Artillery wagon 699053. The photograph was probably taken in 1937; the wagon is in the process of re-painting.

Side view of the artillery wagon 699053 seen from the opposite side.

chassis of the wagons. Both turrets were installed over the bogies. German 7.5 cm *wz. 16nA* guns were replaced over time by standard *wz. 02/26* guns. The turrets of the 699053 wagon were welded; the other wagon had its turrets riveted. The original machine gun turret on the top of the combat compartment of the 699054 wagon was replaced with a standardized anti-aircraft machine gun turret. The same type of turret was mounted on the roof of wagon 699053.

Artillery wagon 699054 being re-painted.

Interior of the "Generał Sosnkowski" turret – there is a slit to the right of the cannon, where a machine gun could be mounted.

The open breech of the wz. 02/26 cannon in the "Generał Sosnkowski" turret.

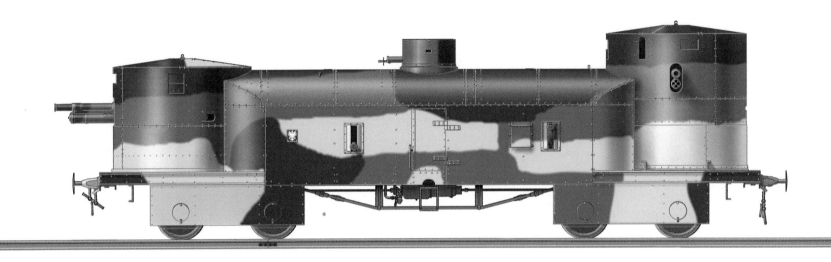

Two profiles of the artillery wagon 699054 – left and right.

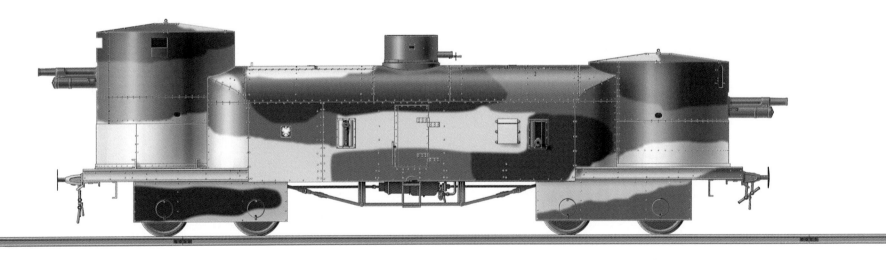

Assault Wagon

The assault wagon of the P.P. 13 had the number 423502. It was a typical example of Polish armoured wagons constructed during the Polish – Soviet war era. Originally, it was the artillery wagon of the "*Stefan Czarniecki*" – with a turret mounting an Austrian 8 cm cannon, and later a Russian 3-inch gun. It was built on a standard German goods wagon chassis with an 8 m long frame and a wheelbase of 4.5 m. The wagon had an unusual observation turret located on the roof, offset to the centre plane of symmetry. The antennae masts were arranged in three rows, four in the outer and five in the middle ones.

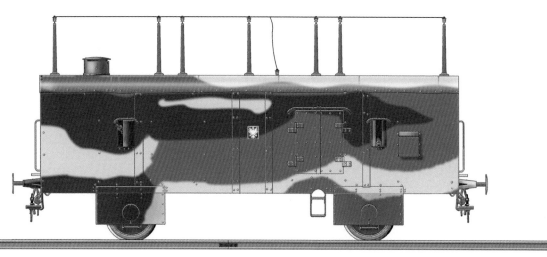

A profile of the assault wagon 423502.

Assault wagon of the "General Sosnkowski" after all modernisation works had been completed – still sporting the experimental camouflage pattern.

Combat Flat Railcars

The front flat railcar of the P.P. 13 was a standardized combat version of the wagon of the *Pdks* series, (Polish type *C-VIII*) with compartments and equipment stowage boxes in the under-frame.

The second flat railcar, the rear one, was also of the *Pdks* series, but it was an ordinary platform, not converted and without a camouflage pattern (in civilian red-brown colour), delivered by *P.K.P.*

Draisine Platoon

The draisine platoon, two *TK-R-TK* sets, originally assigned to the train, was sent to Tczew where it took part in the defence of bridges over Vistula River. The replacement was made up of two *R-Tatra* units.

There is a possibility that there was only one *R* rail draizine (*Renault FT* tank) coupled with two *Tatra* (thus forming a *Tatra-R-Tatra* set).

An assault wagon 423502 – converted from an artillery wagon. The final conversion is not yet complete. The roof section where a gun turret had been originally installed is now covered with an armoured plate. At a later time, profiled and uniform roof segments will be introduced. The heavy machine gun drum will be eventually removed and the exit door will be fitted in this area. Note also a front part of the Ti3-3 locomotive. Picture taken in Mińsk Mazowiecki in the winter of 1931.

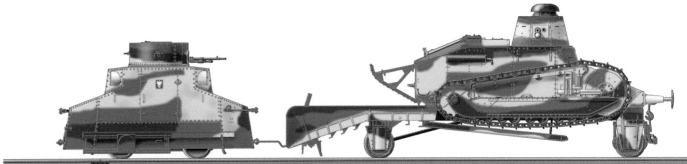

A unique combination of R – Tatra draisine set of the "Generał Sosnkowski".

Administrative Supply Train Section

The support train was probably in par with the established standards – lack of precise information.

"General Sosnkowski" in September 1939

On 1 September the train, commanded by Captain Stanisław Młodzianowski, left Legionowo for Nasielsk. At Nasielsk, the train waited as the army reserve, and it was only on 3 September that it was sent to Ciechanów, where the fighting was escalating. The following day was spent on patrols near Ciechanów. An *R* draizine – tank on the rail guide – was sent on a scouting mission to the Ciechanów railway station. The train was pulled back to the Świercze station, from where the *R* draisine was sent out again for reconnaissance.

In the evening of 4 September, P.P. 13 left for Modlin, where it met the train P.P. 15 – both trains were directed to patrol the area of the Modlin Fortress – the

Combat route of the "Generał Sosnkowski" in September 1939

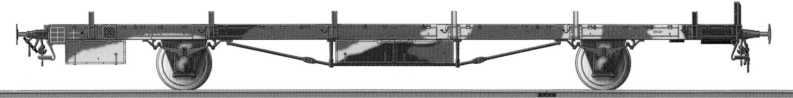

A side view of Pdks flat railcar of the "Generał Sosnkowski" with stowage container in the frame.

"*Sosnkowski*" operated on the Nasielsk – Płońsk line. On 5 September, at the Pomiechówek station, the train repelled an attack by German aircraft.

The morning of 6 September, P.P. 13 left Modlin for Legionowo depot, where it replenished the supplies. On 7 September the train was ordered towards Wyszków – it travelled through the Warszawa-Praga station and along the ring route to Tłuszcz. According to a different account, it travelled via Zegrze and Radzymin, which is more probable. The support train echelon followed.

Afterwords, the P.P. 13 operated near Wyszków. On 9 September it opened fire,

supporting the infantry defending the bridge in Wyszków, and helping to suppress a German attempt to cross the Bug River, in the course of action the train engaged German artillery batteries firing from the Biała Forest.

During the retreat from the Bug River line, on 10 September, the train departed from Wyszków towards Tłuszcz, while the support train section was sent to Mińsk Mazowiecki. The combat section arrived near Łochów around noon of that day with the task of covering the withdrawal of troops. The train crew had to repaired the damaged tracks so in the early afternoon P.P. 13 could continue

towards the crossing over the Liwiec River. At the Łochów station, a heavy bomb dropped from a German plane exploded right next to the track and made a large crater, resulting in the bowing of the rail which caused the train to derail. It is not known whether the engine driver did not notice the crater or took a risk in the hope that he would be able to pass over it.

The story of the P.P. 13 in September 1939 was over a few days later. The crew of the combat section, after leaving the train, marched in the direction of Mińsk Mazowiecki and, not far from Mrozy, joined the support train, which was stuck in track blockages. Four cannons – accord-

ing to another report, six – found in one of the abandoned transport trains made it possible to create a provisional artillery battery which part in the battle at Mrozy.

The later fate of the locomotive remains unknown. It does not appear in the *Ostbahn* or *Wehrmacht* lists – most likely it was not suitable for overhaul and was scrapped. The wagons were not used by the Germans either, although they were transported to the depot of captured equipment on their own wheels.

The derailed "Generał Sosnkowski" in an aerial photograph.

Locomotive, assault wagon and the rear artillery wagon of the derailed "Generał Sosnkowski".
And another aerial view of the "Generał Sosnkowski".

Top and on the left:
The Ti3-3 locomotive.

Below right:
The rear artillery wagon.

On the opposite page:
Photographs of the front artillery wagon.

In both images, the rear artillery wagon may be viewed.

The front artillery wagon – in all photographs.

Top left:
The rear artillery wagon.

Top right:
Part of the "Generał Sosnkowski" combat section set on tracks, and towed to some depot of war loot.

To the right:
Artillery wagon of the "Generał Sosnkowski" – most likely already in process dismantling for scrapping – note the lack of couplings, buffers and the entrance door to a casemate.

On the next page:
A Renault tank and a Tatra draisine set abandoned at Łochów. We are not aware as to the fate of the other R – Tatra draisine set (it is possible it was actually never added the train).

Armoured Train No. 14 (P.P. 3 *"Paderewski"*)

Armoured Train No. 14, P.P. 3 "*Paderewski*" according to old numbering scheme, completed the mobilisation on 4 September 1939.

Locomotive

The locomotive assigned to "*Paderewski*" was a *Ti3* Number 8 (former German engine Number 4114, from the Henschel plant, built in 1904). The tender was of *12C1* type with an unknown number.

The Ti3-8 locomotive of the "Paderewski" entering the station in Toruń.

Combat composition of the "Paderewski" in a photograph taken in 1937. In 1939, it went to war in almost the same composition. The difference is that the photograph both flat railcars are of the modified Pdks type with stowage boxes – in 1939 the train had only one such flat railcar.

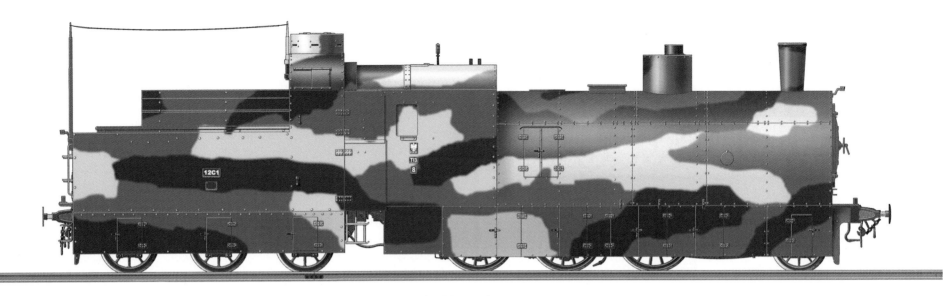

A profile of the Ti3-8 locomotive.

The "Paderewski" locomotive right and left views – cropped and enlarged parts of images.

Artillery Wagons

The wagon 660588 was a front artillery wagon, and number 658641 was the rear one. The new numbering assignment may seem confusing because both original artillery wagons were extensively reworked. In 1933, the superstructures were transferred onto new chassis of American origin, and only parts of the original armour were retained. It resulted in a number change as the number followed the *P.K.P.* scheme and was derived from the characteristics of the undercarriage. The new chassis was a four-axle flat railcar with automatic brakes. The frame was 11.44 m long with a wheel bogie base (Diamond type bogies) of 8 m. Each wagon had a 75 mm *wz. 02/26* gun in one turret and a 100 mm *wz. 14/19A* howitzer in the other.

The artillery wagon 660588 profile.

Artillery wagon 660588 photographed in 1937.

A 100 mm howitzer inside a cylindrical turret of the 658641 artillery wagon.

A memento photograph of the troops of the 1. Dywizjon taken against artillery wagon 658641 in 1935.

Side view of the artillery wagon 658641.

An artillery wagon 658641 in a photograph of 1937.

Guns of the 658641 wagon – upper image a wz. 02/26 cannon, in the lower one a 100 mm wz. 14/19A howitzer.

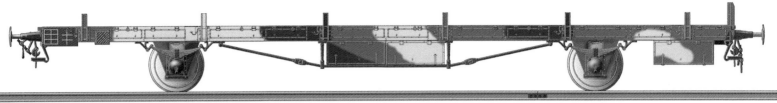

A side view of the Pdks flat railcar with stowage boxes, as used in "Paderewski" in September 1939.

Assault wagon 430044 photographed in 1937.

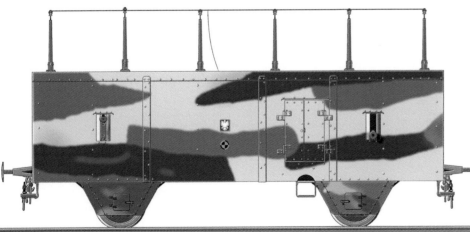

A profile of the "Paderewski" assault wagon.

Assault Wagon

The assault wagon 425627 originally intended for "*Paderewski*" train was actually assigned to "*Danuta*" after its rebuild. So the assault wagon serving with of the Train No. 14 was numbered 430 044. The chassis of the wagon was a typical German coal railcar with a capacity of 20 tons. The assault wagon was a conversion from a single turret artillery wagon serving with "*Stefan Czarniecki*". During the rebuild, the armour of the sides of the wagon did not undergo any significant changes – only the doors were cut out in the armour segments, standardized cylindrical drums for four machine guns were installed, and the lower part of the side armour was reduced to trapezoidal aprons protecting the wheels and their grease-boxes. The rooftop armour plates were completely replaced after the gun turret had been removed. At a later time posts with the antenna were placed on the wagon roof to accommodate the wireless communication equipment.

Combat Flat Railcars

The front flat railcar was a combat version of the wagon of the *Pdks* series with compartments and equipment stowage boxes in the under-frame. The rear one, was also of the *Pdks* series, a civilian version delivered by *P.K.P.*

Draisine Platoon

Two *TK-R-TK* half-platoons each with one *Renault FT* tank and two *TKS* tankettes, as well as an additional *TKS* tankette (including a spare rail guide frame) were assigned to the train.

Administrative Supply Train Section

Probably in par with the established standards – lack of any documentation.

"Paderewski" in September 1939

Armoured Train Number 14, that is pre-mobilisation P.P. 3 "Paderewski", was ready for action on 4 September 1939.

The train, commanded by Captain Jerzy Żelechowski, was initially intended for the reserve of the Commander-in-Chief, but on 1 September a decision was made to assign it to the *Armia "Pomorze"* (Pomerania Army).

On 6 September P.P. 14 arrived at the Kutno station. It probably travelled on a double-track line through Sochaczew (the right side track could still be free from blockage at that time). There is information that it might have gone via Skierniewice, but then it would have to go from Skierniewice towards Kutno on a single-track line, which would have been challenging – thus unlikely.

P.P.14 remained idle for a week at Kutno bombarded by enemy planes. In the interim, Captain Żelechowski was replaced by Captain Henryk Gawełczyk. On 12 September the train was subordinated to the operational group of General Bołtuć and on 13 September it was sent to Łęczyca to support General Grzmot-Skotnicki's cavalry.

On 14 September the train fired its first shots, supporting the *Straż Graniczna* (Border Guard Battalion) in defeating German advance attempt.

Combat route of the armoured train "Paderewski".

The train returned to Kutno and then passed through Rząśno on the Żychlin – Łowicz line. On 15 September it halted at the Jackowice station. The next day it took part in combat action near Urzecze. On the afternoon of that day, the train was attacked by German aircraft, but suffered no damage.

During the retreat of Polish troops to the Słudwia River line, the train was stuck before it could cross the river and had no chance of further withdrawal. The crew left the train, damaging it with the outermost effectiveness. The Germans managed to salvage only the steam locomotive – it was repaired and taken over by the *Wehrmacht*.

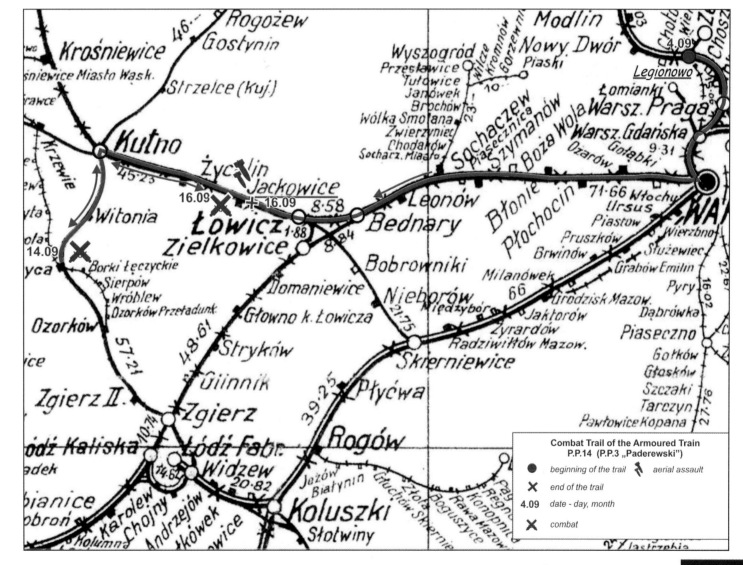

Combat Trail of the Armoured Train P.P.14 (P.P.3 „Paderewski")

● beginning of the trail   ⚔ aerial assault

✗ end of the trail

4.09 date - day, month

✗ combat

The combat section of the "Paderewski" torn apart by internal explosions, shown in an aerial photograph. On the neighbouring track are "cold" locomotives, blocking the track and not yet removed.

The destroyed "Paderewski" and its locomotive. The armour sheets of the front of the engine are scattered around the embankment. Further away, the remnants of the assault wagon may be noted.

In the images on this page, in the foreground, a combat flat railcar and the rear artillery wagon can be seen from different perspectives.

On the next page: Top and below left, the wreckage of completely destroyed assault wagon and the rear artillery wagon, bottom right, a Renault tank demolished by internal explosion and its rail guide.

An R draisine of the "Paderewski". Note, this is a draisine with a wireless set compartment fitted between the ramps.

Armoured Train No. 15 (P.P. 4 "Śmierć")

Locomotive

Armoured Train P.P. 15 completed its mobilisation on 4 September 1939.

The locomotive of the P.P. 4 was a *Ti3* number 5 (former number 4025, Hanomag plant, built in 1904). Tender type *12C1* had an unknown number.

Artillery Wagons

It can only be speculated as to how the combat section of the train was composed in September of 1939. The photographs indicate that the leading artillery wagon equipped with 75 mm cannon had a number 153650 (previously 141455). It came from the Austro-Hungarian armoured train seized in Cracow-Prokocim in 1918. An identical artillery wagon, later numbered 141164 was also captured at the time.

The Austro-Hungarian train acquired in 1918 was divided to form armoured trains "*Śmiały*" (with artillery wagon 141164) and "*Piłsudczyk*" (with artillery wagon 141455). After reorganization, both wagons were assigned to "*Zagończyk*" armoured train in 1919. After this train was decommissioned the wagons were assigned to P.P. 4 "*Śmierć*".

In the background, the Ti3-5 locomotive from the train formed by the 1. Dywizjon to celebrate the ceremonial welcome of the King of Romania, Charles the 2ⁿᵈ – June 1937.

Portrait photograph of the "Śmierć" train as of 1937. In this composition, coupled to the locomotive, artillery wagon 153650. In September 1939, it was replaced by a wagon armed with a howitzer.

The Ti3-5 locomotive. The lightning symbol painted on the steam dome was a warning sign – in those days many lines of the Warsaw railway hub were undergoing electrification, so there was a hazard of high voltage during servicing of the engines.

A profile of the Ti3-5 locomotive.

In both pictures, the welcoming ceremony of King Charles the 2ⁿᵈ and other officials during the visit in June 1937 – in the background is the Ti3-5 locomotive.

The left and right side views of the artillery wagon 153650.

Artillery wagon 153650 in the early 1930's.

A profile of the artillery wagon 141164.

Artillery wagon 141164 in the early 1930's.

Both of the artillery wagons were on the active roster till mid 1930's. Afterwards, the wagon 141164 was placed in reserve. The replacement was a thoroughly rebuilt howitzer wagon, number 430047 (in 1920's it was numbered 248193 and was used by "*Piłsudczyk*" and later "*Gen. Iwaszkiewicz*" armoured trains). Only a slightly modified turret and the chassis of a German *Omku* coal railcar, with a wheelbase of 4.5 m and a length of the under-frame 8.6 m, were retained from the original. The howitzer wagon was positioned as the rear artillery wagon.

The original Austro-Hungarian artillery wagons were also rebuilt – the naval cannon were replaced with an 8 cm field guns due to ammunition availability. The subsequent standardization of artillery pieces – a need to install the *wz. 02/26 75 mm* gun with long recoil presented a challenge. The cradle had to be moved forward so an armoured sponson enclosure had to be constructed to protect the trunnions. The command post superstructures on the roof of the wagons, so-called bastions, were replaced by an anti-aircraft machine gun turret. Heavy machine gun emplacements in the side walls were replaced with retractable sponsons. It was a clever design which allowed the sponson to swivel out and fire the machine gun along the track.

Turret interior with a wz. 02/26 cannon.

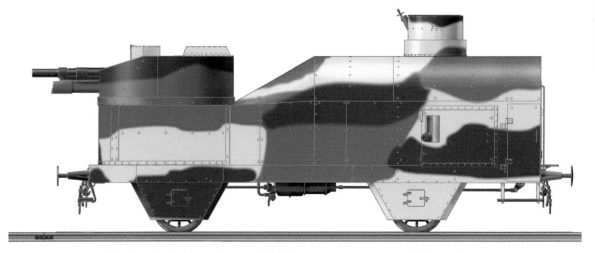

The left and right side profiles of the 430047 artillery wagon armed with a 100 mm howitzer.

Artillery wagon 153650.

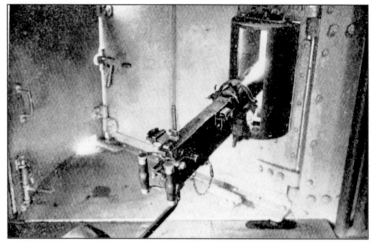

Top and left:
Photographs of retractable
sponson with a machine
gun mounted. Both, wagon
141164 and wagon 153650
had identical technical
solutions.

Assault wagon 390243.

Assault Wagon

Just like the artillery wagons 153650 and 141164, the assault wagon numbered 390243 came from the war booty taken in Cracow-Prokocim. The original Austrian number was S150 060. In the beginning in 1918 it was assigned as an assault wagon in "*Śmiały*", and was later part of "*Zagończyk*" train until its decommissioning. The modernisations included installation of the Westinghouse brakes, replacement of the machine gun emplacements with standard drum mounts, and fitting of a wireless set and the antenna posts.

Combat Flat Railcars

The front flat railcar was a combat version of the *Pdks* series with compartments and equipment stowage boxes in the under-frame. The rear platform railcar, was also of the *Pdks* series, but a civilian version delivered by *P.K.P.*

Draisine Platoon

Unlike all other trains of the 1st Armoured Train Group the No. 15 train was not equipped with *TK-R-TK* draisine sets – it had two *Tatra* draisines instead.

Administrative Supply Train Section

Most likely a typical arrangement – lack of precise information.

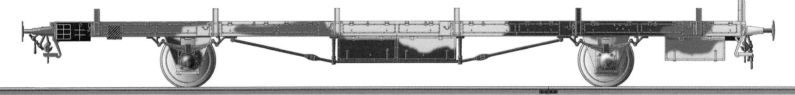

A combat flat railcar of the "Śmierć". Its second flat railcar was of the regular Pdks type, delivered by P.K.P.

"Śmierć"
in September 1939

Armoured Train P.P. 15 completed its mobilisation on 4 September 1939. The train, commanded by Captain Kubaszewski, was originally intended for the reserve of the Commander-in-Chief, but once the mobilisation was completed, it was placed at the disposal of the *Armia "Modlin"*.

On the day of 5 September 1939, the train left Legionowo to patrol the Nasielsk-Ciechanów line. Due to the extensive damage to the track ahead, it was only able to reach Nasielsk – losing the draisine sent further out to scout in front of the train.

On 6 September the train was subordinated to General Juliusz Zulauf, who coordinated the defence on the Bug – Narew River line. From 8 September, P.P. 15 was assigned to the defence of the Modlin Fortress. Damage to the bridge over Bug – Narew resulted in the armoured train being cut off from its support train section – the latter was dispatched to Legionowo, and later to Warsaw.

Rolling stock of the "Śmierć", towed to the Modlin station.

Another view of the rolling stock of the "Śmierć" at the station in Modlin.

When the German siege of Modlin began, the train was stationed within the Modlin Fortress perimeter on a several kilometre stretch of the track between the Modlin station and Pomiechówek. It supported the defenders of the fortress with gunfire, and on 19 September it engaged *Panzerzug Pz. 7* armoured train in a fire fight as the Germans made its approach towards Pomiechówek from the direction of Nasielsk.

On 22 September 1939, P.P. 15 took part in a night infantry attack that eliminated a dangerous breach into the Polish defensive lines. During the following days, the train, hiding in a railway track cutting near Fort Ostrołęka, only rarely opened fire, saving ammunition as supplies were getting low.

On 28 September 1939, there was a truce, and on 29 September the Modlin Fortress surrendered – the crew of the

P.P. 15, having damaged the guns and destroyed their sights, left the train.

The Germans moved the train to the railway station at Modlin. The *Ti3-5* steam locomotive was not fit for repair and was scrapped. The same applies to the combat wagons; they were not used either. The second *Tatra* draisine may have survived, but we are not aware of its fate.

A map depicting the combat route of the "Śmierć".

Combat Trail of the Armoured Train
P.P.15 (P.P.4 „Śmierć")

● beginning of the trail   ⚡ aerial assault
✕ end of the trail
4.09 date - day, month
✕ combat

"Śmierć" train with a howitzer wagon in the foreground.
The Modlin railway station – the gun turret of P.P. 15.

Armoured train "Śmierć" rolling stock towed from Fort Ostrołęka in the autumn of 1939.

On the next three pages: Wagons and locomotive photographed in the winter of 1939/1940. Wagons and flat railcar shunted a little further (damage to the assault wagon's wheel set can be seen). Locomotive still sits in the front of the station building.

A photograph probably taken in autumn of 1939 at Modlin – if correct, we can see the second Tatra draisine of the armoured train "Śmierć".

Top left:
A souvenir picture of the artillery wagon 153650.

A Tatra draisine lost at Nasielsk.

Independent Draisine Platoon of the 1st Armoured Trains Group
(1. Dywizjon Pociągów Pancernych)

In June 1939, a platoon of draisines fielded by the *1. Dywizjon*, was sent out as an independent armoured railcar detachment to strengthen the defence of border bridges in Tczew. It was manned by a cadre platoon of armoured draisines (belonging to the *"General Sosnkowski"* which was considered the cadre training train) supplemented to the full complement by reservists.

The platoon was equipped with two R rail transporters with *Renault FT* tanks and five *TK* rail guides with *TK-3* tankettes. One *R* rail transporter had a metal radio compartment built in-between the ramps with a wireless radio set for communication with the tankettes. Two tankettes were also fitted with radio sets. There was no wireless set in the third tankette. Except the fact that they were eventually lost in action, nothing is known about the fourth and fifth tankettes. The platoon was complemented by two motorcycles (one of them was certainly a *Sokół 1000* with a sidecar which can be seen in a photograph of the unit) a *Polski Fiat 508 Łazik* all terrain car, and a *wz. 34* half-tracked lorry on a rail guide wheels. The images also show *Kd* series covered wagons – probably a small support section accompanying the platoon of draisines. After the engineers had blown up the bridges and the defence troops had been withdrawn, in the evening of 1 September the platoon left for Tczew – the equipment, after having been damaged by the personnel, was abandoned by the crew probably near Toruń.

An abandoned draisine platoon near Toruń. It was formed by the 1. Dywizjon Pociągów Pancernych. *On the tracks, a* wz. 34 *half-tracked lorry on a rail guide, next a TK-3 tankette on a rail guide, then an empty TK rail guide. Behind them is an R transporter with a* Renault *tank, followed by two rail guides with TK-3 tankettes fitted with wireless sets. The last armoured draisine is an R transporter with radio compartment and a* Renault *tank. In the very rear there are four or five Kd series covered goods wagons.*

TK-3 *tankettes fitted with wireless sets. Between them the wreckage of the Sokół 1000 motorcycle with a sidecar.*

A Renault FT *tank with an old pattern serial number (1050) painted on the running gea*

In the top images, the TK-3 rail guides photographed after the Germans had towed away the remaining elements of the unit. A radio compartment can clearly be seen on the Renault's rail transporter.

To the left:
An R tank on a rail transporter – the radio compartment was placed between the ramps. Unfortunately, the compartment is out of frame of this photograph. In the 1. Dywizjon, there were two such equipped tank transporters, the second one set off to war with "Paderewski".